Awesome Yo-Yo Tricks

Shar Levine &
Bob Bowden

Main Street
A division of Sterling Publishing Co., Inc.
New York

The Library of Congress has cataloged the previous edition as follows:

Levine, Shar, 1953-
    Awesome yo-yo tracks / Shar Levine, Bob Bowden
    p. cm.
    Includes index.
    Summary: Presents the history of the yo-yo and describes the basic
    techniques involved in simple, intermediate, and advanced tricks.
    ISBN 0-8069-4468-4
    1. Yo-yos-Juvenile literature. [1. Yo-yos.] I. Bowden, Bob II. Bowden,
Robert, 1954- III. Title.
    GV1216.L48 2000
                    99-051642

10 9 8 7 6 5 4

This edition published in 2005 by Sterling Publishing Co., Inc.
387 Park Avenue South, New York, NY 10016
© 2000 by Shar Levine and Bob Bowden

For information about custom editions, special sales, premium and
corporate purchases, please contact Sterling Special Sales
Department at 800-805-5489 or specialsales@sterlingpub.com.

Sterling ISBN 1-4027-2898-0

Dedication

For Jeff Connery. Thank you for your kindness, generosity, friendship, talent, and for always doing wonderful work under the most trying of conditions. As always, thanks to Paul, Shira, and Josh.

—*Shar*

For my son, Dominic, who brings joy and laughter into my life and who makes it all worthwhile.

—*Bob*

As always for the two women in my life, my daughter and my mom.

—*Jeff*

A great big "I love you" to my big brother Torben and to my Mum and Dad, Caroline and Ole. You're the best!

—*Emily*

Acknowledgments

As always there are many people to thank. If we forgot someone, we're terribly sorry. Thanks to:

American Yo-Yo Association
Harvey Lowe
Andrew Phillips, for taking time out of his
   schedule to go on a scavenger hunt.
NASA
Joel Zink and his family
Yo-Yo Museum, and especially Bob Malowney
   for his assistance
Josh, Shira, Maryanne, Mat, Liz, and Dominic
   for volunteering on a cold, wet Saturday.

Contents

Introduction

You are about the learn the ins and outs of one of the world's oldest toys—the yo-yo, also known as the return top. Why "return top," you may ask? Simple. For many years the word "yo-yo" was owned by the Duncan Company. This meant that other names for the toy had to be created. For that reason, "return top," "spinner," "yo," "bandalore," or any of a number of words involving "yo" could be found adorning the face of the toy.

Everywhere around the world, children love yo-yos. By using this book you, too, can become an expert in the art of yo-yoing. It will take some practice, some patience, and, preferably, a large, empty space for you to become a spinning pro.

Much like playing marbles, yo-yo tricks and techniques have developed over many years. While some tricks are known by standard names, others have tags specific to different regions or areas. To con-fuse matters even more, various yo-pros—the people who do this for a living—may even create and name a trick. Some names, such as "Spank the Baby," may offend people, so these traditional tricks will be called by their new names.

You can even study with the masters. Check with the American Yo-Yo Association to see if your city has a yo-yo clinic. You can even obtain instructional videos. These can help you perfect even the toughest of throws.

This book is designed for the beginner. Once you have mastered your throws, you can move on to more difficult maneuvers. The tricks are classified within each section: a trick with one yo-yo ( ) is the simplest. Two yo-yos are intermediate. Three are advanced, and four are for experts only.

Now, grab your favorite yo-yo and get started!

Who is this tiny person and what is she doing here? See page 82 for an explanation.

Safety First

Yo-yos are not meant for small children. A child under the age of six generally does not have the eye-hand coordination necessary to operate the toy. In young children's hands, a yo-yo simply becomes a weapon on a string. We recommend that children be at least seven before being given yo-yos.

Yo-yos can do serious damage to walls, windows, lamps, vases, TV sets, stereos, and computer screens (not to mention animals and small children at ground level). Here is some basic advice:

1. Measure the length of string on your yo-yo. Add to that the length of your arm when fully extended. This will give you your "circle of danger." No one and nothing should stand within your "circle of danger." Don't forget to look up when measuring so you don't damage light fixtures.

2. Make sure you use your yo-yo in a wide-open space, away from any objects, people, or animals. The last thing a parent wants to hear while you are playing with your toy is a crash, followed by the word "oops." Do not play with your yo-yo near small children or animals.

3. Make sure your yo-yo is securely attached to your finger.

4. If you hurt yourself or someone else, tell an adult immediately. You

Arm extended

can get a nasty concussion if you aren't careful or even a huge black eye. A misplaced throw can knock out teeth, so play carefully.

5. Don't throw a yo-yo at your pet pooch to make your dog fetch the wooden ball.

6. Never turn your yo-yo into a weapon by sharpening the edges, adding studs, or doing anything else that could make it dangerous!!

7. If you happen to break something, the word "yo-yo" takes on new meaning: "You're On Your Own."

Arm upwards

History of Yo-Yos

Where the Name Is From

If ever a toy suited its name, it's the yo-yo. The folklore and even some dictionaries record that the word "yo-yo" means "come back" and is perhaps derived from Tagalog, a language in the Philippines. This relative of the yo-yo would not have been fun to play with, as it was actually a weapon. A long rope was attached to a huge yo-yo that had jagged edges and sharp spikes. The warriors could either swirl this weapon at their opponents or launch it through the air, hauling it back in if the shot missed its target. This impressive story has no basis in fact.

Another theory, popular with some longtime yo-yo experts, is that the history of the yo-yo was fabricated by a sharp marketing guy who needed a convincing tale to explain where yo-yos came from. This marketing "spin," so to speak, has now become part of yo-yo history.

Yo-Yos through the Ages

Imagine a child dressed in a toga standing in front of the Oracle of Delphi playing with a yo-yo. While the image may seem a little strange, this is how far back the yo-yo dates. While there are better designs and materials today than 2,000 years ago, the basic toy hasn't changed much. The idea is to join two halves of a disk in the middle, tie a string to this joint, and make the disks go up and down. (It sounds so easy, doesn't it?) Ancient versions were made of clay, wood, or even metal. Much like the modern yo-yo, these were decorated toys with pretty designs or patterns.

Modern Yo-Yos
(warning: puns to follow)

This toy has had its ups and downs in popularity. Not to string you along, but yo-yos have been going around the world for hundreds of years. In the late 1700's the fad spread from Asia to Europe and quickly became a hit in all social circles. Yo-yos finally reached the United States in about 1860, where the practice of Bandalore soon grew to immense popularity then fell out of fashion and became a sleeper.

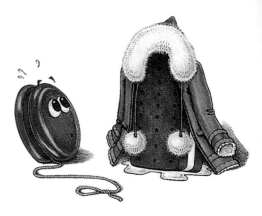

Bandalore

The Boy's Modern Playmate, written by the Reverend J.G. Wood and published in England in 1895 by Frederick Warne and Co., had this to say about yo-yos: "About the beginning of the present century (the 1800's) the bandalore became suddenly a fashionable toy under the name of Quiz, and scarcely any person of fashion was without one of these toys." In other words, yo-yos were so popular in England, reference was made to them in children's books.

Flores Yo-Yo Company

Back to its southeast Asian roots, a Filipino immigrant named Pedro Flores started a small factory in California. He called his gadget a "yo-yo" and by 1920 was soon producing these novelties en masse. Which is where the story really takes off.

Duncan

What do Eskimo Pies, Good Humor Ice Cream trucks, parking meters, four-wheel hydraulic brakes, and yo-yos have in common? Quite a bit, it seems. Donald F. Duncan Sr, the man who made yo-yos a household word, was in some way responsible for all these everyday items. Duncan, a wealthy industrialist, knew a good thing when he saw it. In the late 1920's he heard about the success of this tiny factory in California and he liked it so much, he bought the company. Duncan acquired the Flores Yo-Yo Company, copyrighted or legally protected the term "yo-yo," and the rest is history.

Antique yo-yos

Playing with yo-yos is a great stress reliever. French nobility were seen toying with their "Joujou de Normandie" on their way to the guillotine. The rich and noble who wanted to continue to play with their yo-yos fled to Koblenz, Germany, where the toy soon became known as "l'émigrette" (the emigrant) or the Coblenz, in honor of its new home.

Not only was Duncan a genius when it came to inventions, he was ahead of his time when it came to marketing and promotion. He arranged a partnership with a newspaper chain. In exchange for free advertising in the paper for his yo-yos, Duncan agreed to have each entrant in his contests bring in several new subscriptions to a Hearst newspaper. This campaign was so successful, at one time the Duncan factories were actually producing over 3,600 yo-yos per hour. To give you an idea of the power of this type of advertising, Duncan sold over 3 million units in 1931 in a one-month promotion in Philadelphia.

In Search of the Perfect Yo-Yo

As the saying goes, "Build a better mouse trap and the world will come knocking on your door." In this case, Dr. Tom Kuhn wanted to build a better yo-yo. Motivated by the fact that he had a broken yo-yo, Kuhn soon set to work creating the perfect top. He carefully crafted some of the world's most beautiful wooden tops. Not content to manufacture collector's yo-yos, he soon began designing and innovating new designs. He perfected the first take-apart yo-yo with reversible sides. He also popularized aluminum yo-yos. He is also a co-holder of a patent for a ball bearing transaxle system with adjustable gaps. His designs enabled other yo-yo manufacturers to improve on basic yo-yo mechanisms.

Yomega

By the mid 1980's, yo-yos were in need of some scientific change. Along came a "yo-yo with a brain," from Yomega. This yo-yo is different because it doesn't rely on the basic string on an axle to make it go up and down. Instead it has a special mechanism that the yo-yoer can view through the see-through plastic casing. This mechanism makes it easier for a beginner to perform basic tricks. It is also faster than the yo-yos most people grew up playing with. The actual name for the guts of this toy is "centrifugal clutch." This yo-yo is different from traditional ones in a number of ways. In the Yomega, friction inside has been reduced, so the yo-yo spins longer. This is done with the use of a free spinning nylon spool on the axle. The rubber ring on the end of the axle is grabbed by the clutch as the yo-yo begins to slow down. The clutch "compresses" and forces the yo-yo back up into the yo-yoer's hand.

Aluminum yo-yo

TRIVIA

Check your calendar and mark off June 6th. It's been designated "National Yo-Yo Day," in honor of Donald Duncan Sr.'s birthday!

DID YOU KNOW

The yo-yo is the second-oldest toy in the world, the doll probably being the oldest. What about marbles, you may ask? Well, while marbles date back to the time of the pharaohs in Egypt, they are a game, not a toy. So there.

Yomega yo-yo

Types of Yo-Yo

Have you ever looked at a yo-yo closely? If you turn a wooden yo-yo on its side you can see there is a subtle difference between yo-yos. These styles affect the ease with which you can perform tricks.

Price Doesn't Count

Is a more expensive yo-yo better than a cheap one? Yes and no. Before purchasing a yo-yo to play with, you should consider the fundamental components that a decent yo-yo ought to have. A bottom-of-the-line dollar or novelty yo-yo will not be the easiest to learn on. It's better to start with a yo-yo that retails for about $7. It's not necessary to spend over three times that amount for a yo-yo that will allow you to learn tricks easily.

Even the experts have favorites and prefer one style over the other. Some yo-yos work better for certain tricks and others are easier at certain levels of play.

Competitive yo-yoing

Try Before You Buy

When purchasing a yo-yo, see if the store has a demo model you can test drive. Choose the best one for you. Or try out a friend's yo-yo and see if it is the one for you!

Imperial

The Imperial is the most common and recognized yo-yo shape. This shape was the one first used in the United States. It has a rounded surface on the outside and the inside is a flat plane.

Butterfly

This yo-yo gets its name because it looks like a butterfly from the side. It was first made popular by Duncan in the mid 1950's. This yo-yo is basically an Imperial top turned inside out. The rounded edges are on the inside of the yo-yo, while the outside is now a flat plane.

Modern/Modified

What would happen if a termite ate away part of your yo-yo? You'd be left with something like the modern version of a traditional yo-yo. This design, also known as a "rim weighted" shape, was first developed in the early 1970's by Donald Duncan Jr. What is so interesting about this particular yo-yo is that most of the weight is on the outside edge. What this means technically is that the shape increases the "rotational inertia," thereby permitting longer spin times. (For

Inexpensive
plastic yo-yo

Various yo-yos

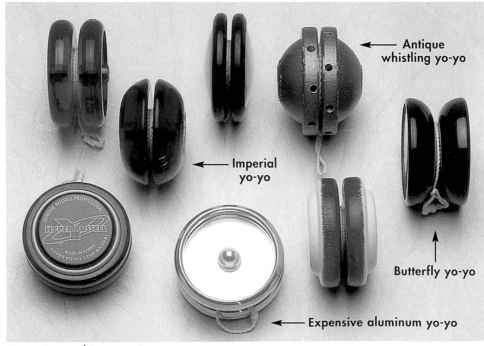

Antique
whistling yo-yo

Imperial
yo-yo

Butterfly yo-yo

Expensive aluminum yo-yo

Expensive and inexpensive yo-yos

more about why yo-yos work, see "The Science of Yo-Yos," page 33.)

The yo-yo looks like an Imperial from the side, but head-on you can see that the inside section has been hollowed out. Some modern yo-yos have extra weights which you can add to help you perform tricks. Usually only experts put these weights on their yo-yos.

Holographic

Some yo-yos have holographic disks covering hollowed-out sides. The purpose of the disks is more than making the yo-yos prettier and advertising the manufacturer. The disks hold weights in place so they don't go flying off during tricks. Unless you know what you're doing, it's not a great idea to remove these disks.

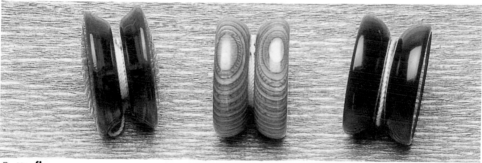

Butterfly yo-yos

Closed and opened rim-weighted yo-yos, sometimes referred to as "modified" or "modern" styles. Note the washers.

Novelty Yo-Yo's

As strange as this may sound, some yo-yos aren't meant to be yo-yos. Novelty yo-yos are oddly shaped. They may look like turtles, snakes, footballs, or even billiard balls. These yo-yos are fun to collect but will not perform the same way as a traditionally shaped toy. If you are a beginner, do not purchase one of these yo-yos to learn on. They are not easy to use to perform tricks.

Blue yo-yo with white weight

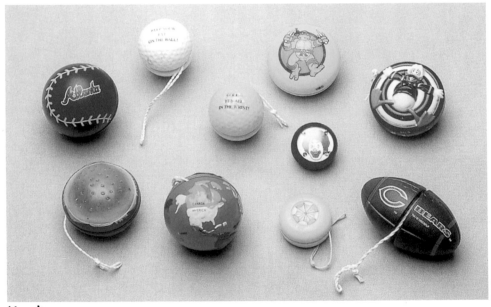

Novelty yo-yos

With hundreds of yo-yos on the market, how do you choose? Next time you can get to a yo-yo competition, talk to the participants or judges and get their opinions! Watch out for so-called "experts" on the Internet. Some may be sponsored by certain companies, so they only promote their sponsor's brand of yo-yo. Other sites may offer advise given by novices. They may not have the expertise to give you the information you need.

Axles

Regardless of the shape, yo-yos all have one thing in common—they have an axle. The axle holds the two halves of the yo-yo together. Without this, you'd be left with a wooden hockey puck and a piece of string. Axles come in different sizes—the thinner the axle, the more friction or energy in the spin. The wider the axle, the less energy. There are two main categories of axle in yo-yos: fixed-axle yo-yos and transaxle yo-yos. This is important to know, because axle type affects the tricks you perform and how long your yo-yo will last! For example, the type of axle on your yo-yo will determine the amount of time your yo-yo "sleeps." Assuming identical string tension, if a fixed axle sleeps 15 seconds, a sleeve transaxle might sleep up to 45 seconds, and a bearing transaxle could sleep over a minute. Of course, your mileage may vary, because throw is just as important as axle type when timing a sleeper.

Fixed Axle

Take a close look at the guts of your yo-yo. If it just has a solid piece of wood or metal doweling holding the two sides together, and the doweling doesn't have anything sitting on top of it, then you have a yo-yo with a fixed axle. Don't try

Hockey puck and yo-yo

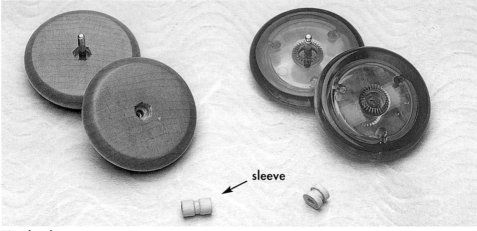

Fixed axle

to twist the yo-yo apart as not all fixed axles can be opened. Most, in fact, are glued together. This is the traditional or old style of axle where the string slides directly over the axle.

Transaxle

If your yo-yo doesn't resemble the one above, then you have a transaxle. Take another look at the insides of your yo-yo. It will have either a sleeve or a bearing over the axle.

Starburst

With a sleeve system a small plastic ring covers the axle, and the string fits over this ring. This plastic sleeve will now spin freely around the axle. A yo-yo using this design can spin up to three times longer than a fixed-axle model.

Another type of transaxle yo-yo uses a ball (or roller) bearing. With this type of transaxle, the string is attached to the outer face of the bearing. This bearing can spin

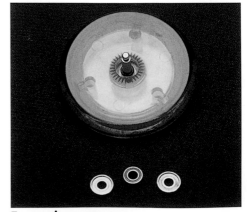

Transaxle yo-yo

Transaxle yo-yos

freely while the inner face is solidly mounted to the yo-yo. The ball bearing axle spins even longer than the sleeve transaxle yo-yo.

Variations on a Theme

Some yo-yos have "starbursts" on the inside of the yo-yo body circling the axle. These are slightly raised or bumpy grooves on the plastic. The purpose of this is to create a "positive grip" for the string to grab onto when you want the yo-yo to return.

If you listen carefully, you can hear the sound of a ball bearing transaxle yo-yo. It is similar to the old, open bearing roller skates or certain kinds of in-line skates.

DO NOT OPEN

The only time you need to take your yo-yo apart is when you have to fix the axle or the bearings or untie a knot in your string. It is easy to "strip" the axle by frequently unscrewing and reassembling the two sides of the yo-yo. The bottom line is: don't open the yo-yo if you don't need to.

Maintenance or Fine Tuning

A yo-yo can last many years if you take care of it. Keep it in top working order just by following these few simple steps:

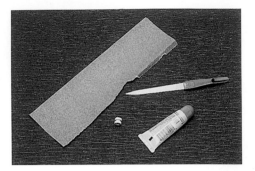

1. If the wooden axle looks shiny and worn or a groove has begun to wear into the wood, it's time for repair. If it's the kind that can be replaced, put in a new axle. If it isn't, take off the string and, using a toothpick, place a drop of water on the wooden groove.

2. If you have a take-apart yo-yo, use fine sandpaper and gently smooth the axle, but not too much, however, or you will ruin it. If you have rough surfaces on the wooden axle, use a nail file to smooth out the spots carefully. A nail file can also be used to remove excess glue from the axle. Caution: a nail file can easily scratch or gouge the axle. If this happens, it's time for a new axle.

3. Some people adjust the "gap" between the two sides of the yo-yo. If the space between the two sides is too narrow, it can be changed by adding a special spacer to the axle. If the gap is too large, the axle can be shortened or

changed. Generally, fiddling with the axle is not recommended, and you might wish to purchase a new axle if you have the replaceable kind.

4. If your transaxle yo-yo doesn't return, it may not be a tension problem. The bearing or sleeve may just be too dry. It is simple to fix this. On this occasion, it is permissible to take apart your yo-yo to lube or oil these kinds of axles. Some experts recommend lip balm to condition these bearings. Add a dab to each side of the bearing or on the axle of a sleeved yo-yo. Take care not to get any lube on the threads of the axle itself. If this happens, the yo-yo could come apart while in use. Put the yo-yo back together, and you're on your way. Mineral oil, baby oil, or household oil with a non-stick coating also work fine.

Yo-Yo Maintenance

Everything You Need to Know about Strings and Knots

One of the most important components of your yo-yo is the string. Here are a few things you need to know about string:

1. Yo-yo string needs to be changed after about three hours of use.

2. Don't throw away your yo-yo when all you need is a new string.

3. Change the string if it looks dirty or frayed or it just doesn't seem to be working right.

4. Use "soft" string made of cotton. "Hard" synthetic string is not the string of choice for real yo-yo enthusiasts.

Take a moment to look at your string. It's not like the string used to tie boxes. Yo-yo string is a long piece of cotton thread twisted and wrapped back up in a double length. It is tied at the end to give you a loop that you use to create a slip knot for your finger.

New strings and old used ones

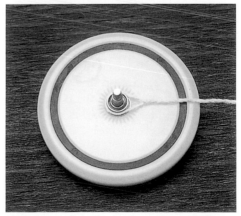

String on a bearing transaxle yo-yo. Notice the loop on the axle.

Try This

Find an old yo-yo and take it apart. Using regular household string, tie a knot around the axle. Reassemble the yo-yo and try to throw a Sleeper. (See instructions, page 45). You will find this trick impossible to perform! Remove the string and try it again with yo-yo string. Your yo-yo should sleep like a baby.

This helps explain why yo-yo string looks the way it does. A yo-yo doesn't rise and fall on a string. It rolls up and down on the inside of a loop! When the loop has the right tension, the yo-yo will go down the string and the axle will spin inside the loop. The yo-yo will then wind itself back up the string

HOW TO REPLACE A STRING

Contrary to what's done in schoolyards across North America, it's not necessary to take apart a yo-yo in order to change the string. In fact, it's not any more necessary to take apart a yo-yo to change the string than it is to remove the engine from a car to rotate the tires! To remove a yo-yo string, simply hold the yo-yo by the string and spin it to the right, or in a counterclockwise direction. This will loosen it until it forms a wide loop that you can slide off the axle. Take a moment to check the axle and make sure it's in good condition.

Make sure you know the kind of axle your yo-yo has, because stringing varies depending on the type.

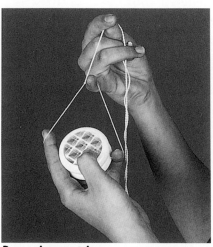

Removing a string

To begin, take a new string and unwind it about 5 inches (10 cm) from the looped end. Untwist the string by turning it to the right, making an opening about 1 inch (2.5 cm) larger than the diameter of the yo-yo. This next part is tricky.

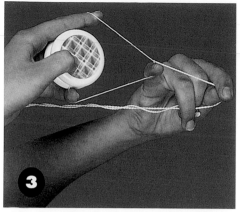

Open the loop to create a slip knot that can fit any finger.

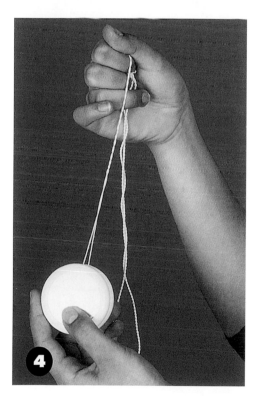

How to Put the String on a Fixed-Axle Yo-Yo

Many beginners use a "double loop" of string around their axle. It isn't necessary. To string your yo-yo, simply do this:

1. Take a new string and unwind the looped end enough to be able to fit your yo-yo through the opening.

2. Insert your yo-yo through the opening, then drop the yo-yo onto the string, so the string rests on the axle. Give the string one twist or rotation.

3. When the string is in place, hold the yo-yo by the tied end and allow the yo-yo to spin.

4. Give the yo-yo a clockwise spin to adjust the tension, and you're ready to rock and roll.

How to Put a String on a Transaxle Yo-Yo

Transaxle yo-yos can spin using single, double, or even triple loops around their axles. Single loops are advisable for smooth tricks, such as Braintwister (page 76). Two or three loops are better for looping tricks. Since you can find many different models of transaxle yo-yo on the market, follow the manufacturer's recommendations for best results. Basically, you load your string as follows:

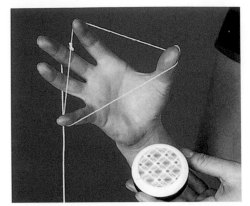

A new string for the yo-yo

1. Take a new string and unwind the looped end enough to be able to fit your yo-yo through the opening.

2. Drop the yo-yo onto the string so that the string rests on the sleeve or bearing. Make sure the string is on this piece, or your yo-yo won't go anywhere.

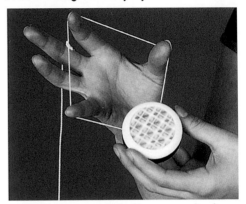

Give the yo-yo one half turn, so the front side faces the back.

3. Pass the yo-yo back over the string again, through the loop to create the "double loop." Make sure the string stays on the sleeve each time you loop the yo-yo.

4. For a triple loop, perform step 2 again.

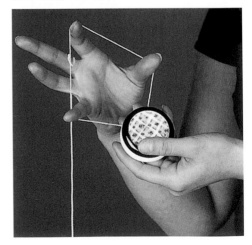

5. When the string is in place, hold the yo-yo by the tied end and allow the yo-yo to spin.

6. Give the yo-yo a clockwise spin to adjust the tension, and start your tricks.

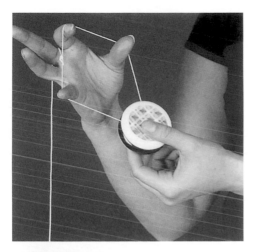

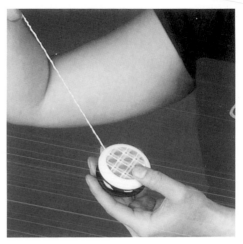

Incorrect way to tighten a yo-yo

Putting it Back Together – Tightening

If you took your yo-yo apart to perform any maintenance, i.e., oiling the bearings, you have to be careful putting it back together.

Try this: Place your palms flat on either end of the flat part of the yo-yo. Gently rotate your palms in opposite directions until your yo-yo grips. Don't squeeze the two sides together, as you will "strip" the axle! Over-tightening will ruin your yo-yo.

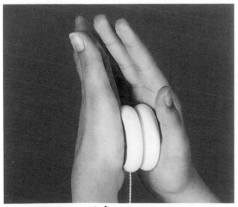

Correct way to tighten a yo-yo

Waxing a String

Some yo-yoers insist that adding a dab of wax—such as paraffin from a candle or beeswax—to the last few inches of the string (the part next to the axle), improves their tricks. If you surf, the kind of wax you put on your board is perfect for this. WARNING: If you think you have enough wax, it's probably too much. Excess wax will make a great sleeping yo-yo that is almost impossible to wake up.

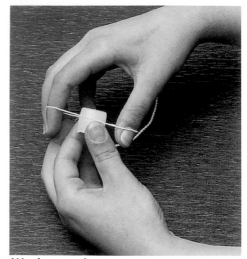

Waxing a string

String Problems and How to Solve Them

A guy walks into a psychiatrist's office and says: "Wigwam. Teepee. Wigwam. Teepee." And the psychiatrist tells him: "You're two tents" (too tense). This brings you logically to the next section, which is about yo-yo tension.

If the string on your yo-yo is too loose, the yo-yo won't do tricks like "hop the fence." If the string is too tight, it won't sleep. And sometimes your string turns into a wiggly worm or spaghetti and won't return your yo-yo, at all.

String tension (left to right: too tight; just right; too loose)

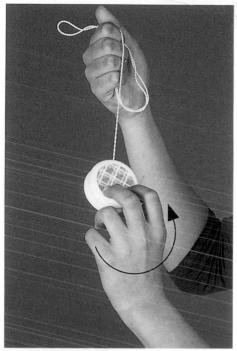

Spinning to the left

Here are some ways to change the tension of your string:

To loosen the tension, spin your yo-yo to the left.

To tighten the tension, spin your yo-yo to the right.

To untwist, hold the yo-yo and allow the string to fall to the ground. This should allow the string to return to a more useable state.

To untie a knot: If the string is really knotted, take it off and get a new one!

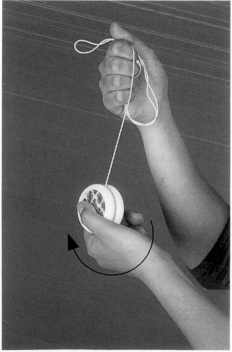

Spinning to the right

Trading and Collecting

Hold on to that yo-yo of yours! Some day it may be worth money. Yo-yos are sought-after collectors' items. Books, magazines, and auctions are devoted to yo-yos and yo-yo paraphernalia. An original Flores from the 1920's can sell for over $300.

The Science of Yo-Yos

Next time your parents catch you playing with your yo-yo instead of doing homework, you can simply explain that you are working on a science project. Yo-yos are a great way to study physics. In particular, yo-yos can teach you about gyroscopic stability, friction, air resistance, potential and kinetic energy, and precession. And don't forget rotational inertia!

If you're not into science, just skip this section. But if you'd like to know what's happening when you yo-yo and why, keep reading.

Yo-yos have a mind of their own, physically speaking. When they are thrown in one direction, they want to stay moving in that direction. This is called inertia. If the yo-yo is spinning in one plane, it wants to stay spinning in that plane. This is called rotational inertia. For example when you throw a flying disk it wants to stay in the same plane, so it flies flat. If you throw a flying disk in such a way that it doesn't spin, it would tumble, roll, and not go very far. When you do a trick like a Sleeper, if you throw it off your fingers straight, it stays straight; if you throw it crooked, it spins crooked and comes to a stop. When you do a trick like Man on the Flying Trapeze, the yo-yo goes straight until you use your finger to change the direction the yo-yo is moving in.

If a disk that is spinning has a weight in the middle, it won't spin well because all the weight is on the axle. If you put weights on the outside of a circle, it will spin faster. The further the weight is from the center, the longer it will spin. This is called the distribution of mass and explains why yo-yos are shaped the way they are. A hollow top yo-yo will therefore spin longer than a solid one because it has a higher proportion of the weight distributed on the circumference of the disk.

As you know from school (or will when you get older), energy is never created or destroyed; it only changes form. Potential energy is "stored energy," whereas kinetic energy is "moving energy." Got that? If I take a rubber ball to the top of a 10-story building, it has potential energy (from gravity). When I drop it, the potential energy is converted into kinetic energy as it moves faster and faster until it hits the ground. Then its kinetic energy is converted again into heat, sound, and some is again stored as another type of potential energy (elastic).

Now, what does this have to do with your yo-yo?

When you wind up the yo-yo, it also has potential energy. As it rolls down the string it has kinetic energy. This is again reconverted to potential energy as it winds back up the string.

The friction of the yo-yo going up and down the string converts some of the kinetic energy to heat and sound. Because this energy has been converted to heat and sound, the yo-yo begins to slow down. You need to add more potential energy either by winding it up again or getting it to spin faster.

Compare a yo-yo to a gyroscope. You probably think these two toys are very different. A gyroscope looks like a blending of metal disks. To get it spinning, you wind a string around the shaft and set it loose. Once spinning, it can be raised off a surface and made to balance at different angles while perched on a string. If the gyroscope is spinning fast enough, it will try to "right" itself, so it doesn't fall off the string. As you change the angle of the string, the gyroscope will adapt its angle to the string and miraculously hang on for dear life.

Now, can you make a yo-yo do the same thing?

Try This

Throw a Sleeper in such a way that it tilts or leans to one side. The string will rub on the inside rim of the yo-yo. This should slow the yo-yo down. What else does the yo-

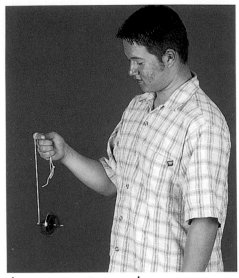

A gyroscope at an angle

yo do? As it turns out, the yo-yo wants to lean in the direction which it is tilting. The term in physics for this is "precession."

If you have a yo-yo that is weighted, remove the weights from one side. Throw a Sleeper. Your yo-yo should now be doing a great example of "precession." This means that your yo-yo will turn toward the side that is the heaviest or is weighted, but it will not "tip" over. The yo-yo will spin to the left when tilted to the right or spin to the right when tilted to the left.

What does all this mean to you? Well, there are only so many things you can blame on a yo-yo, when a trick doesn't work. My yo-yo isn't balanced is one of them. It's simple to determine if that's a problem with your yo-yo. You can tell if one side is heavier if when you drop the yo-yo it twists to one side.

A Bit of History

In the old days, yo-yos were made of one piece of wood, which was lathed into the familiar yo-yo shape. Today, yo-yos are constructed of three pieces: two sides and the axle, which is glued in place. Barney Akers, one of the legendary demonstrators for Duncan yo-yos, used to keep factory "seconds." These yo-yos were the end of the run, which meant that one side was larger than the other. In other words, the two halves were different sizes. One would be a normal size; the other would be about half the diameter. Whenever a child complained that his yo-yo wasn't balanced, Barney would pull out his bizarre lopsided yo-yo and proceed to do tricks with it.

Did You Know

NASA wondered if it was possible to yo-yo in space. On two missions, one on April 12, 1985, and the other on July 31, 1992, astronauts practiced yo-yo tricks. What did they learn? For one thing, yo-yos won't sleep in outer space. They also discovered that a yo-yo doesn't go anywhere without gravity--you had to throw it.

Photo courtesy of NASA

Yo-Yo Info On-Line

NOTE TO PARENTS

The Internet is a great source for information. It is recommended that you place child-protection programs on your Internet connection. It is also recommended that you supervise children while they are online. You don't need to sit with your children, but you should be in the room and check from time to time on the appropriateness of the sites. Make certain your children do not give out any personal information when posting messages to forum sites. Finally, remember that some of the information on the Internet is anecdotal. That is to say, it may not always be correct. If you are uncertain about the accuracy of any material, check it against another source.

Anything you need to know about yo-yos is on the Internet. Use any search engine, type in the word "yo-yo," and soon you will have more information than you can handle. Some sites feature animated pictures of tricks, while others have hints about how to do the latest tricks.

The authors of this book have their own websites. Find Bob at www. intergate.ca/personal/bobb/yo.html. His site features the best in yo-yo information and links to other safe sites.

Check out Shar's website. It's at www.sciencelady.com. She has cool stuff from her books and also science gossip. Check out both sites.

Yo-Yo Master-Harvey Lowe

There are legends in every sport and Harvey Lowe is certainly one of the most famous yo-yoers. A hearty 80-something-year-old who lives in Vancouver, B.C., Canada, Harvey is a sought-after celebrity in the art of yo-yoing. Back at the first world championship, held in England in 1932, Harvey walked away with the trophy. Because Harvey's heritage is Chinese, he is frequently and incorrectly referred to as the "Chinese Yo-Yo Champion." In fact, he's Canadian. Lloyds of London even insured his hands for over $150,000! Young yo-yo enthusiasts travel from all over to learn from this master.

Young Masters

Would you like to spend eight hours a day perfecting your yo-yo tricks? That's how Joel Zink, a young yo-yoer from Reno, Nevada, occupies his day. A straight-A student, Joel specializes in free-style yo-yoing. When he is not in school, he travels the country with his parents and brother, Ryan, who also is an up-and-coming yo-yo star, performing in various competitions, where he is clearly a crowd favorite!

Joel Zink in competition

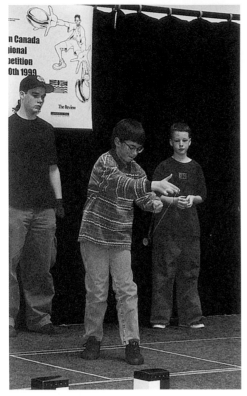

Ryan Zink in competition

National Yo-Yo Museum

Next time you're in Chico, California, check out the National Yo-Yo Museum. Eighty years of yo-yo artifacts are on display. A good time to visit this fascinating museum is when the National Yo-Yo Championships are held, usually in the fall. This competition has thousands of entrants at all levels of ability.

The museum features the collection of the D.F. Duncan family, and has wonderful examples of early Duncan, Cheerio, Festival, Royal, and Flores yo-yos. Have your picture taken next to the world's largest yo-yo, which weighs in at 256 pounds and stands over 50 inches in height.

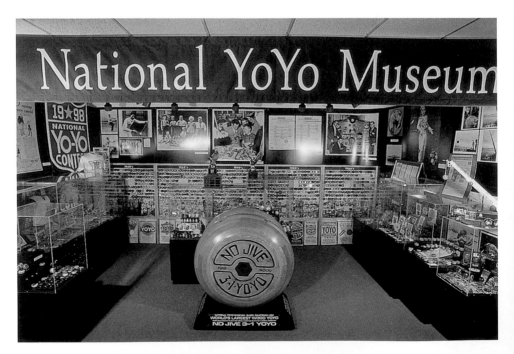

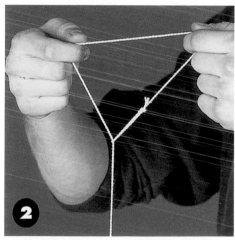

Yo-Yo Basics

Now that you know all the parts of the yo-yo, you're just about ready to learn the art of yo-yoing. But you're not there just yet.

How to Put a Yo-Yo on Your Finger

Thanks to yo-yo string manufacturers, you can easily tell which end of the string is which. The part with the tied loop is the top and the other end is the bottom that fits around the axle. DO NOT put your finger through the loop! Instead, run part of the string back through the loop to create a "slip knot." Place your middle finger through this slip knot and tighten it so it won't slide off. The string should be about halfway between your first and second knuckle.

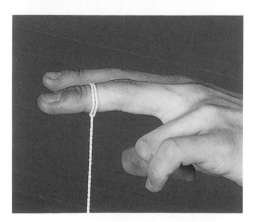

How Long Should My String Be?

Place your finger in the slip knot loop and let the yo-yo fall to the floor. Hold your hand even with your navel. If your string is the correct length, it should just graze the floor. Unless you are over five feet tall, chances are you will need to trim the string. With the yo-yo on the floor, measure the string 3 inches (7.5 cm) above your navel and cut the string. Tie a knotted loop, just like the one you just cut off, then run a slip knot back through the string.

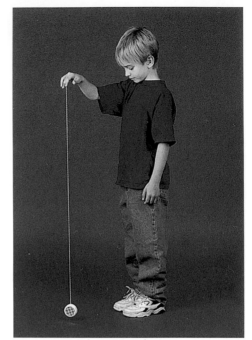

Yo-yo string that is too long

Now What?

Wind the string back into the yo-yo. For looser tension, wind the string toward you. For more tension, wind the yo-yo away from you.

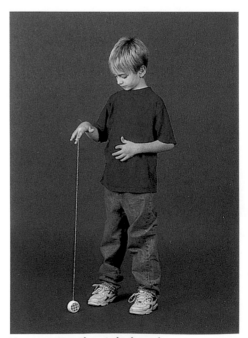

Yo-yo string the right length

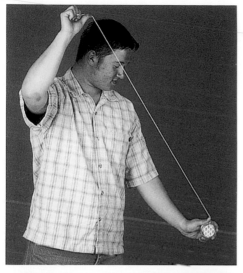

Thumb Wind

One way of getting a string around a yo-yo is called a thumb wind.

1. Place your yo-yo hand up above your shoulder, about even with the top of your head.

2. Place the thumb of your free hand in the space between the two sides of your yo-yo. Your thumb should be pressing forward into the string. Hold the bottom end of the yo-yo with your pointer finger.

3. Pull the string taut between your two hands.

4. To get it to wind back up, push down with your thumb and lift with your yo-yo hand at the same time. The yo-yo will not come all the way up, but you can dribble it up to your hand using several up-and-down motions.

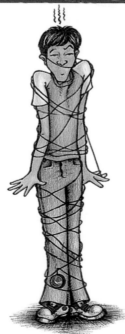

Plan B

1. Another variation of the thumb wind is to use two fingers wrapped around the string. Use your fingers to spin the yo-yo out, pushing downward while pulling the string up.

If All Else Fails

Hold the yo-yo in your free hand. Leave plenty of slack and wind the string up around the yo-yo.

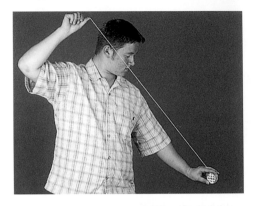

Holding a Yo-Yo

This is probably intuitive, but just in case it's not, here goes: Put the string on your finger. Cup the yo-yo in the palm of your hand so that the string winds around the top of the yo-yo and goes toward your finger.

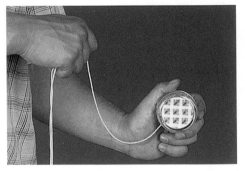

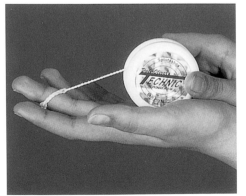

Yo-yo held the right way

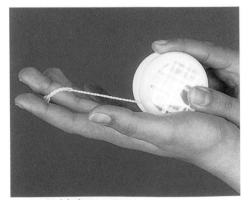

Yo-yo held the wrong way

Basic Throws

This is probably the first trick most beginning yo-yoers attempt.

1. Hold the yo-yo in your hand with the palm facing down. Release the yo-yo and let it fall toward the floor.

2. As it travels on its downward journey, follow it down with your hand.

3. Just before the yo-yo gets to the bottom of the string, raise your hand. This will make the yo-yo climb back up the string. When it gets to the top, catch it.

Alternatively, instead of catching it, see how many times you can make it go up and down. This trick is called the Dribble.

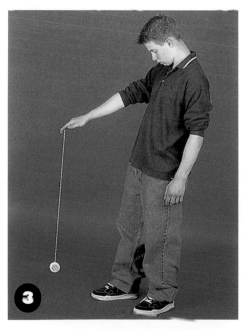

Basic Power Throw

1. Cup the yo-yo in your palm and lift your elbow high enough that it is even with your eyes.

2. Throw your arm forward and let the yo-yo roll off the end of your fingers. Do not turn your hand over until the yo-yo is completely out of your hand.

3. Turn your palm downward, and lift your string finger. The yo-yo will return to your hand.

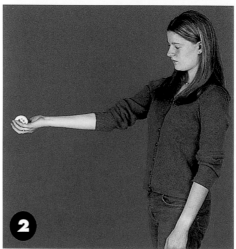

Remember: In all throws, use only one hand to catch the yo-yo. Try not to have any more than 3 inches (7.5 cm) of string left over between your yo-yo and your finger.

Sleeper or Spinner

Shakespeare once wrote "to sleep, perchance to dream," but not about playing with a yo-yo. This is one of the fundamental yo-yo throws.

Note: You can vary the length of time a yo-yo will sleep by the manner in which you throw it. The more powerful a throw, the longer it will sleep and the more it will spin at the bottom of the string. A gentle throw will result in a slower spin at the bottom of the string.

1. First check the tension of your string. If you think your yo-yo is too tight, hang it and give it several spins to the left (remember right-tight, left-loose). This trick works best with a loose string and a looser loop on the axle.

2. Cup the yo-yo in your palm and lift your elbow high enough that it is even with your eyes.

3. Throw your arm forward and drop the yo-yo. Your yo-yo should be spinning at the bottom of the string.

4. When you want your yo-yo to return, turn your palm down, lift your string finger, and the yo-yo will return to your hand.

Forward Pass

Unlike a football quarterback, you won't have to worry about anyone catching this pass.

1. Cup the yo-yo in your palm loosely. Do not hold on to it. Make sure you keep your palm facing backward and your knuckles forward as you move your arm behind you. This is the same motion you use when you go on a brisk walk.

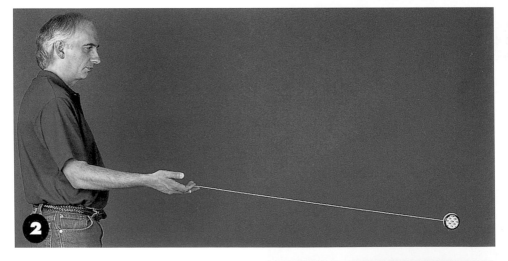

2. Release the yo-yo as you swing your arm forward. Bend your elbow slightly at the same time, so your elbow ends up about waist level. Turn your palm upward.

3. The yo-yo will shoot out in front of you and return to your hand.

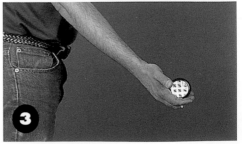

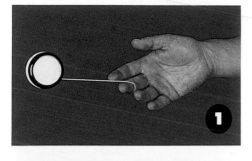

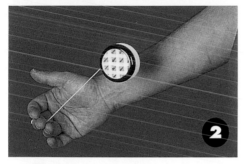

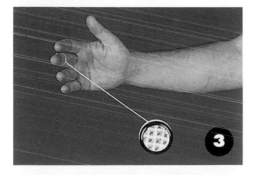

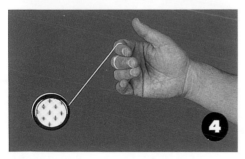

Note: In competitions, Loop the Loop is frequently used to break ties. Competitors can do 200 or more in a row.

Loop the Loop

Not to get too loopy, but this is really fun to do.

1. Throw a forward pass.

2. Just before the yo-yo returns to your hand (where you would normally catch it), twist or rotate your wrist to send the yo-yo forward again. It is the same wrist motion as when you wave at someone to come closer.

3. The yo-yo should pass on the inside of your body. Try to get one good loop. When you can do one, try doing two, then try for five. Keep doing this until you can do 20 in a row. Remember to practice only good loops. If you lose control of your loops, stop and start again.

4. As you get better, practice alternating the loops. Do one repetition with the yo-yo on the inside of your body, with the next on the outside of your body.

Loop the Loop with a strobe yo-yo

Beginner Tricks

Rock the Baby

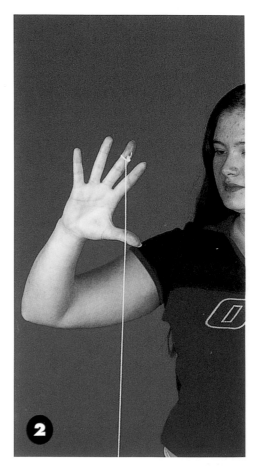

There are a number of versions of this trick. This one is the simplest way of doing this classic. Some people mistakenly call this "Rock the Cradle." We'll show you that version, too.

1. Throw a fast Sleeper. You need to keep it sleeping long enough to do this trick.

2. Hold your yo-yo hand out as if you were asking someone to "stop." You should have a flat palm facing forward with the yo-yo string against your palm.

3. Take your free hand and pull the string between your first finger and thumb of your yo-yo hand, toward your body.

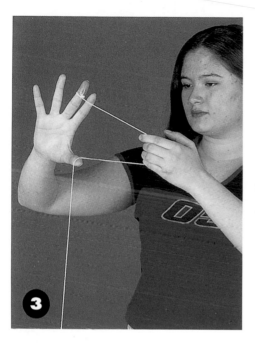

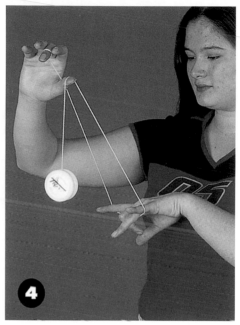

4. Use your fingers on your free hand to split open the string into a triangle shape. It should be wide enough for the yo-yo to be able to swing freely between the strings. You can size the cradle easily using this method, so you will always have sufficient space in which to swing. Move your top hand slightly to cause the yo-yo to move in and out of the triangle shape. This is the "rock."

5. After several passes through the archway release the string, and the yo-yo will wind up into your hand.

The Famous "Rock the Cradle"

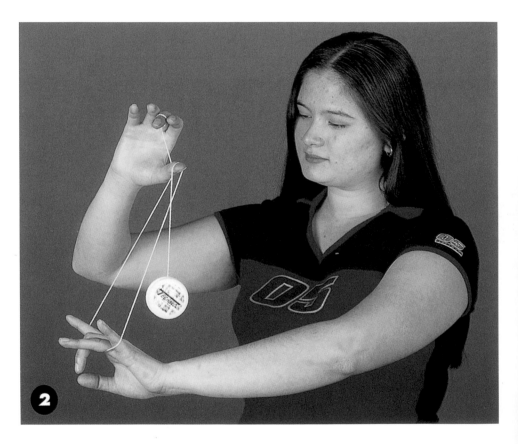

Perhaps it's because the English language is such a precise tool that this trick was created.

1. Complete all the steps in "Rock the Baby," but do not move the yo-yo in and out of the archway.

2. Instead, use your bottom or free yo-yo hand to move the triangle back and forth.

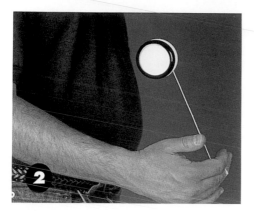

Hop the Fence

You won't have any major physical exertion with this next trick. Your wrist will substitute for a picket fence.

1. Do a basic power throw.

2. Instead of catching the yo-yo as it returns to your hand, slightly flick your wrist forward, as if you were pushing on a joystick, so the yo-yo does a flip and is propelled back down the string.

3. Practice till you can do this 10 times in a row. Catch the yo-yo on the last flip.

Walk the Dog

Here's one pet you won't mind taking out.

1. Throw a basic Sleeper. You might want to throw a fast one as it will work better.

2. When the yo-yo begins to sleep, bend forward slightly and allow the yo-yo to just touch the ground.

3. Keeping the yo-yo string taut, move your hand slowly forward, allowing the yo-yo to spin along the ground.

4. When the yo-yo has traveled about a foot or so away from you, yank the string and catch the yo-yo in your hand.

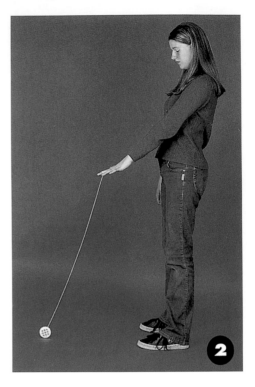

Breakaway

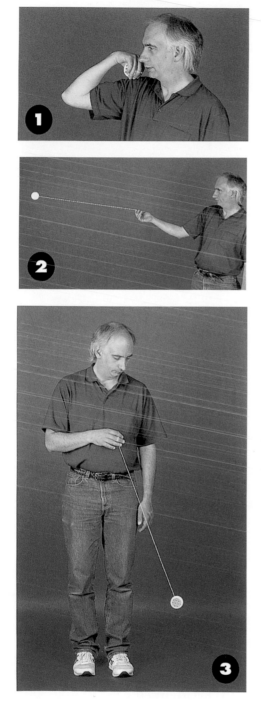

Your yo-yo may look as if it were trying to make a run for it, but unless your string breaks, this one will come back!

1. Make a muscle (like a weight lifter) by lifting your arm sideways. Your elbow should be even with your shoulder and the yo-yo should rest on your shoulder. Curve your wrist downward away from you.

2. Flip your arm straight, releasing the yo-yo as you do this. The yo-yo will swing out and should now be soundly sleeping.

3. In one smooth motion, your hand will naturally move downward, then across your body. The weight of the yo-yo will cause it to swing across in front of your body.

4. As the yo-yo completes its arc, give the string a tug with your yo-hand and it will snap back into your hand.

Around the World

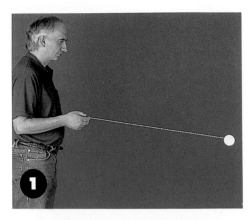

In his classic book, Around the World in Eighty Days, *Jules Verne described the difficulties of making a journey such as this. You won't have half the problems his characters did, as you attempt to do such a feat with a yo-yo.*

REMEMBER: Look up and check for low-lying light fixtures before doing this trick.

1. This first step may seem counterintuitive—that is to say, it may seem to make no sense and may go against what you'd normally think of doing. Throw a hard Forward Pass aiming slightly downward. Your yo-yo should be sleeping.

2. Pretend you're walking. Swing your arms in a natural motion, with the palm of your hand facing behind you. Just as you are moving your arm from back to front, let go of the yo-yo.

3. When your arm has reached the front of your body, stop your swing and allow the yo-yo to continue its journey around the world. You don't need to move your arm in a circular motion as if you were doing a "back stroke" in swimming.

4. When the yo-yo has completed its loop, give it a small yank to return it to your hand.

Advanced

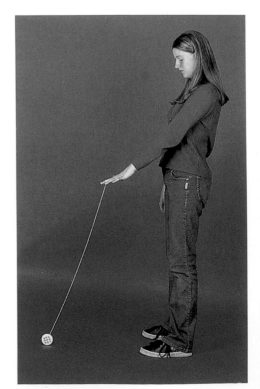

By now you've impressed your friends and family with your new-found talent. You're ready for some more challenging tricks.

Creeper

This is not a trick involving climbing ivy, nor is it a scary movie. It's a variation of Walk the Dog, but your string will be parallel to the ground. Here are two of the several versions of this trick:

1. Throw a basic fast Sleeper.

2. When the yo-yo begins to sleep, swing the yo-yo out in front of you and let it land gently on the floor.

3. Give the string a tug, and the yo-yo will come back. Remember that the yo-yo must stay on the floor for its entire trip back to your hand.

Creeper II

This second variation is commonly called Land Rover.

1. Throw a basic fast Sleeper.

2. This time when the yo-yo begins to sleep, bend forward at the waist and knees until your hand is just above the floor. The yo-yo should be scooting along the ground away from you.

3. As the yo-yo reaches the end of the string, give it a tug, and it will come shuffling back.

Around the Corner
(also known as Over the Shoulder)

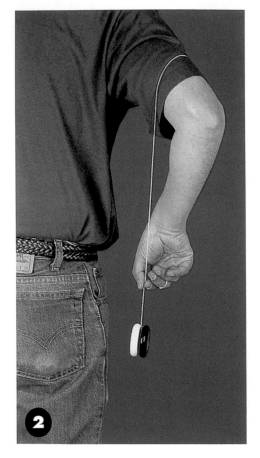

This one looks great. If you do this in a competition, make sure to roll your sleeve so the yo-yo doesn't get caught in the material.

1. Throw a basic fast Sleeper.

2. Lift your hand straight up and allow the yo-yo string to go behind you and rest on your shoulder.

3. Lean slightly forward so your fingers on your yo-yo hand can touch the string on your shoulder.

4. "Pluck" or tweak the string and the yo-yo will climb back up the string, flip over your shoulder, and land back in your hand.

Over the Falls

There's no water involved here.

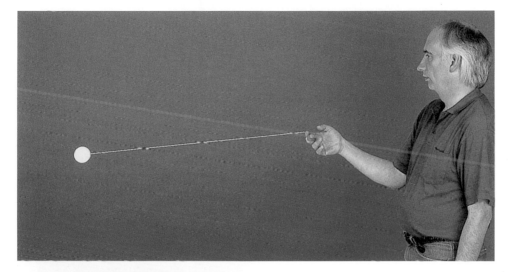

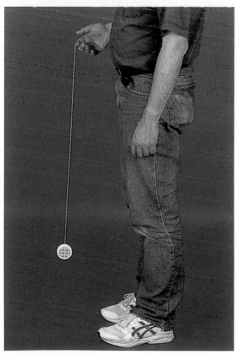

1. Throw a Forward Pass. Remember to use the same arm motion you would if you were swinging your arms while walking.

2. Before the yo-yo gets back to your hand, curve your wrist and allow the yo-yo to drop to the ground.

3. Catch the yo-yo as it returns to your hand.

Punching Bag

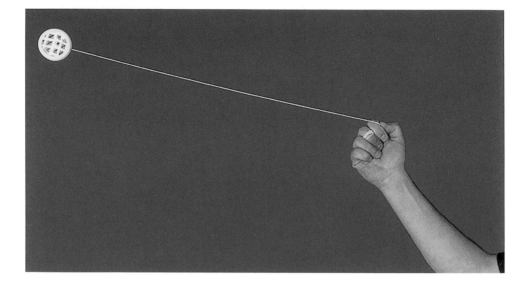

Boxers practice by hitting a punching bag. It looks like a puffy basketball hung on a string and suspended above the ground at head height. Here's the yo-yo equivalent. This trick is to make the yo-yo do something it doesn't want to. It has to do a reverse loop. The yo-yo has to go in a direction from the top of the yo-yo toward the bottom, as opposed to bottom or under the hand, as in Loop the Loop.

1. Check the tension on your string. You want it tight, so the yo-yo doesn't sleep in the middle of this trick. Begin by doing Hop the Fence. As the yo-yo hops over your hand, gradually raise your arm and force the hops to go in a horizontal direction in front of you. The secret is to already have good control when Hopping the Fence.

2. For a single trick, catch the yo-yo as it returns to you.

3. When you can perform this without any difficulty, try to keep the yo-yo punching the air repeatedly. Try doing two, then try for five. Keep doing this until you can do 20 in a row. Remember to practice only good loops. If you lose control of your loops, stop and start again. Keep in mind that this is one of the hardest looping tricks in existence, so don't feel bad if you can't get the hang of this right away.

Three-Leaf Clover

Not as lucky as a four-leaf clover, but a lot more fun. The key to this trick is to know how to count to three. Don't laugh: Many people in yo-yo competitions get this one wrong. You will be throwing a combination of an Inside Loop, followed by an Over the Falls.

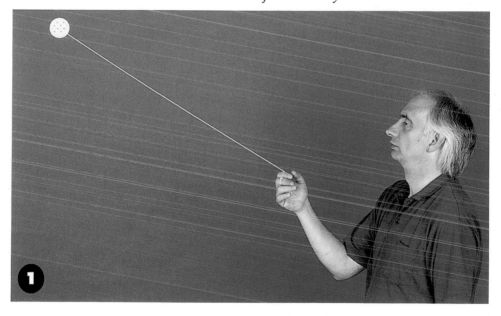

1. Check the tension on your string. You want it tight, so the yo-yo doesn't sleep in the middle of this trick. Instead of throwing a Loop in front of you, aim upward at about a 45-degree angle, then throw your Loop. This is the first leaf.

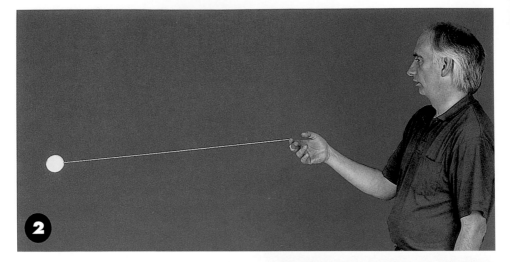

2. This next step is basically the same as Over the Falls. As the yo-yo returns, flip your wrist so the yo-yo does a turn and heads straight out from your body. This is the second leaf.

3. Just as the yo-yo returns, flip your wrist again and head the yo-yo toward the floor. This is the third leaf. Catch the yo-yo when it comes up. Try to make the yo-yo go straight down on this last leaf.

Flying Saucer
(Sleeping Beauty)

As you use your yo-yo, the string gets tighter or looser. One way to adjust this tension is to perform this trick.

1. Place your arms at a 45-degree angle to the side of your body. Throw a Sleeper at this angle.

2. When the yo-yo is sleeping, use your finger to draw up the yo-yo string to a horizontal position in front of your body.

3. The yo-yo will begin to "vibrate" or spin sideways (horizontal to the ground). You will actually see the string spinning sideways around the yo-yo.

4. Give the string a slight tweak up with your free hand. As you do, the string will wind back up into the yo-yo.

Lariat

You won't catch any horses with this variation on the Flying Saucer, but you should be able to rope in your yo-yo.

1. Throw a Sleeping Beauty, but do not use your free hand to lift the yo-yo by the string.

2. Instead of grasping the string with your free hand, move your yo-yo hand from the 45-degree angle to a position directly above the yo-yo.

3. Pull the yo-yo straight up and move your hand to the side as it rises. You should see the string rotating around the yo-yo as you do this.

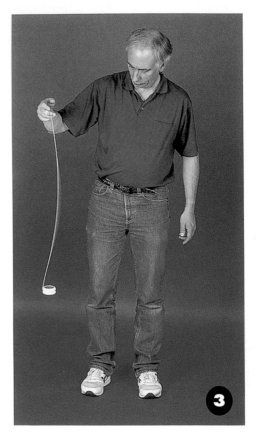

Rattlesnake

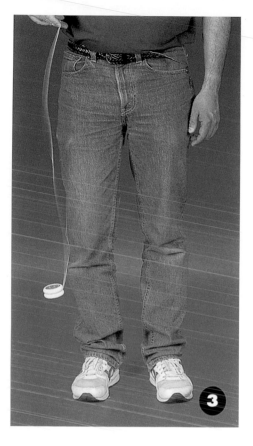

You won't get bitten by this snake, but you will really see why this trick is named after a reptile. It is recommended that you wear long pants while you perform this trick.

1. Throw a Lariat (see above).

2. As the string is oscillating above the yo-yo, bring the yo-yo back toward your leg.

3. Allow the string to barely touch your leg. This will give you the sound of a rattlesnake.

Man on the Flying Trapeze

🚩 🚩

This is a classic yo-yo trick—the quintessential string trick—and one that never fails to impress people. You may see yo-yo experts wearing one glove that looks eaten away by moths. The glove is used to cut down on rope burns from tricks such as this.

1. Throw a Breakaway.

2. With your free hand (the one without a yo-yo attached to it), put your pointer finger in a direct line with the arc of the yo-yo string. Make sure you put your finger about 2-3 inches (5-7.5 cm) away from the end of the yo-yo. If you do this too close, the yo-yo will bite your finger. If you are too far away, the yo-yo will probably miss the string and go around your finger.

3. The yo-yo will flip over your finger and land on the string.

4. Bring your hands slightly together, then pull them apart. As you do this, the yo-yo will "dismount" and wind back up into the toy. This is usually called the "flyaway dismount."

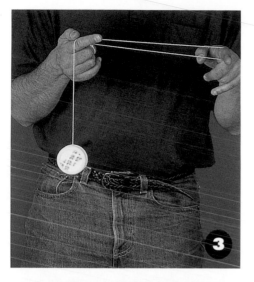

Double or Nothing

This trick gets its name because if you do the throw correctly it will loop twice, but if you miss, you end up with a dangling string—in other words—nothing.

1. Throw a fast Breakaway.

2. As it completes its arc, place your finger out to the side (as you did in Man on the Flying Trapeze). Instead of catching the yo-yo on the string, allow the yo-yo to continue traveling until it reaches your yo-yo hand.

3. Point the index finger of your yo-yo hand outward and allow the yo-yo to swing over that finger.

4. As the yo-yo passes the yo-yo index finger allow it to catch onto the string and flip over. The forward momentum of the yo-yo should land on the string.

5. Release the yo-yo using a "Fly Away" dismount and catch it as it returns.

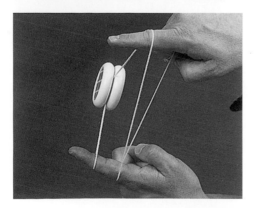

Triple or Nothing

Allow the yo-yo to continue one more rotation around your hand before catching it on the string. As in Double or Nothing, if you miss, you'll end up with a mass of string and a yo-yo going nowhere.

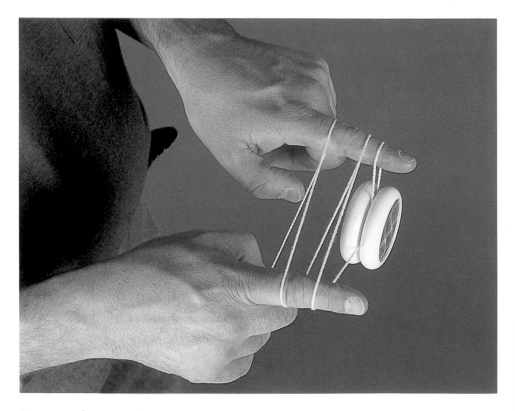

Hint: Each time the yo-yo wraps around your finger, the string should angle off the other end. The string should not be parallel when viewed from above. Remember that the yo-yo's final landing will be on the outside string.

Pinwheel

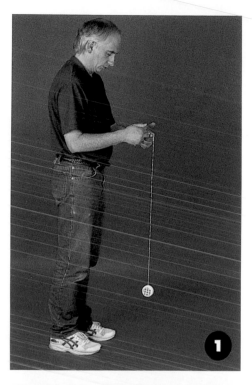

Pinwheels are something you normally use to catch the wind. This pinwheel won't do that, but you'll see why it is so named. There are a number of variations on this trick. This is the one asked for in competitions.

1. Throw a fast or strong Sleeper. This should be thrown directly in front of your body.

2. Using the thumbnail of your free hand, place the fingernail in front of the string. (Why the thumb nail, you may ask? To save you from string burn!)

3. Pull down with your yo-yo hand, and raise the yo-yo to about shoulder level.

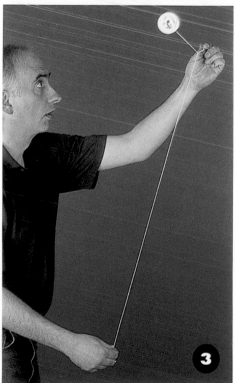

4. Pinch the string with your thumb and index finger of your free hand.

5. This pinching, along with the spinning of the yo-yo, will allow the yo-yo to rotate several times around your hand.

6. Drop the yo-yo and it will return.

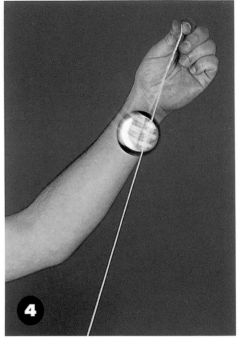

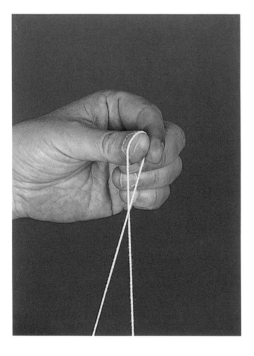

Variation:

If you don't pinch the yo-yo, but just allow it to rotate around your index finger, it will come off your thumb and onto the finger, then drop. This is called a "Pull Over."

Tidal Wave

This is the new name for what has traditionally been known as "skin the cat," which, of course, no one should ever do. While tsunamis (large tidal waves) aren't much fun, Tidal Wave is a better name for the trick.

1. Throw a fast or hard Sleeper.

2. Place the pointer finger of your free hand behind the string. Pull the yo-yo hand back toward your side in a downward motion.

3. When your yo-yo gets to about chest level, give the string a light flip with your pointer finger. The yo-yo will pop up and return to your hand.

4. Instead of catching the yo-yo, give your wrist a twist and send the yo-yo outward. It will resemble a loop and will be at waist level, not ground level.

5. As it returns this time, catch the yo-yo in your hand.

Expert

Reach for the Moon

🚩 🚩 🚩

This tough trick gets its name because it is as ambitious as reaching for the moon.

1. Start with a Forward Pass, but aim this one about 45 degrees up, so your throwing hand is about as high as your nose.

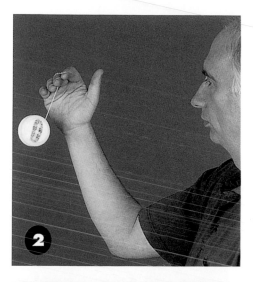

2. As the yo-yo returns to your hand, give your wrist a slight flick, so the yo-yo passes under your hand and continues up and behind you.

3. When the yo-yo comes back down and is about the same level as your hand, give your hand a forward wrist flick and send the yo-yo back up into the air in front of you.

4. If you are just doing one repetition, catch the yo-yo on its return. Remember one repetition is "front, back, front, catch."

5. If you are doing several repetitions, keep flicking your wrist as you did in steps 2 and 3. Expert yo-yoers can do at least 10 of these in a row.

Planet Hop

On the subject of objects in space, here's another one that's out of this world. Don't confuse this with Hop the Fence.

1. Start with your Basic Power Throw.

2. As the yo-yo returns to your hand, allow the yo-yo to hop over the top of your hand.

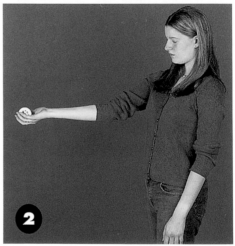

3. When the yo-yo comes back up again, give it a slight flick (as in Hop the Fence) and it will jump back over your hand. One repetition is "front, back, front, catch." Hop the Fence is a loop going in only one direction. Planet Hop alternates between front and back.

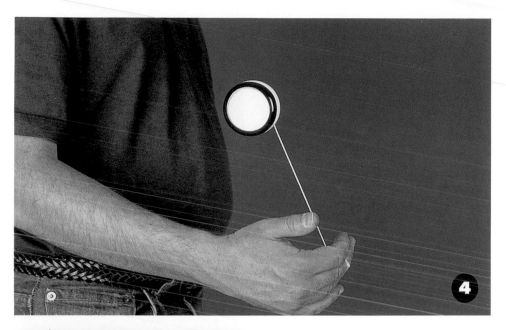

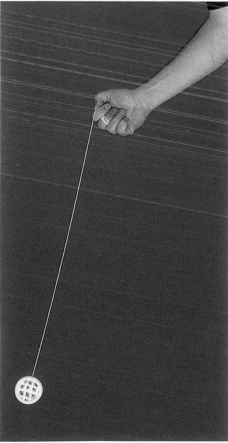

4. Try to see how many good reps you can do in a row. Remember to start over when you lose control.

Brain Twister

🚩 🚩 🚩

Wrap you mind around the next trick. A word of advice: Wear a glove and keep your free hand as steady as possible.

1. Throw a fast or hard Sleeper.

2. Place the index finger of your free hand about halfway down the yo-yo string.

3. Pull back to lift the yo-yo with your finger so it is about even with your chest.

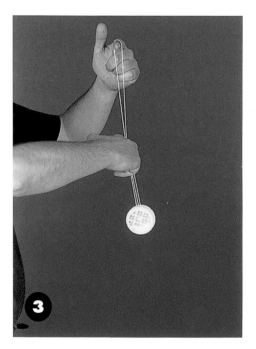

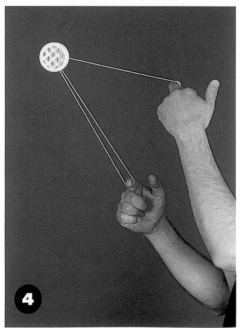

4. Slip the yo-yo onto the string, about halfway between this finger and the finger the yo-yo is attached to.

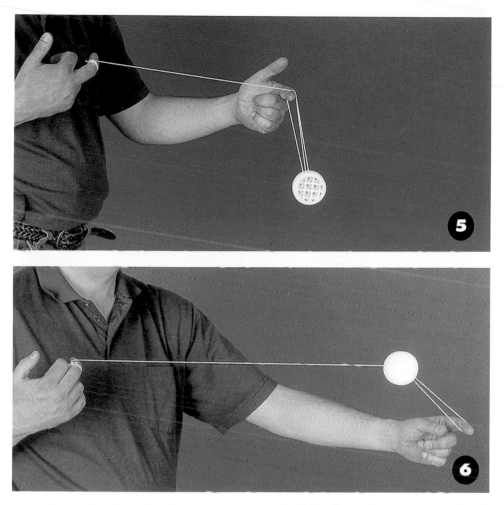

5. Adjust the length of string by bringing your yo-yo hand about halfway between the yo-yo and your non-yo-yo finger.

6. Use your yo-yo finger to push back into the double string and guide the yo-yo, so that it somersaults over your non-yo-yo finger.

7. Pull back with your yo-yo hand and release the yo-yo, so that it rolls off and returns to your hand.

Atom Smasher

If you had a particle accelerator handy you could use it, but a yo-yo will work just fine. This is the toughest one-handed string trick you will have to do in most competitions. Good luck! By the way: this is the basic version—there are harder ones.

1. Throw a fast or hard Sleeper.

2. Place the index finger of your free hand about halfway down the yo-yo string. Pull back to lift the yo-yo with your finger until it is about waist level.

3. Tuck your yo-yo finger into the palm of your hand, then use your index finger to flip the yo-yo string onto the finger. The yo-yo will hop over your finger and onto the string. This is called a "split bottom entry." Do not punch the string as you will probably miss the hop. The weight of the yo-yo will be enough to carry it forward.

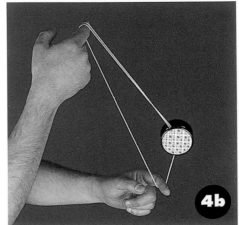

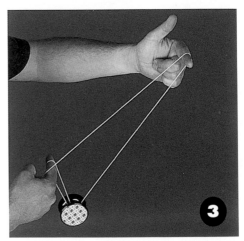

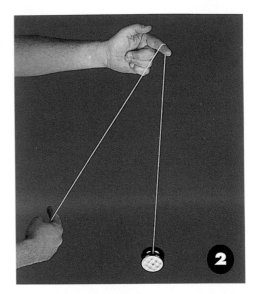

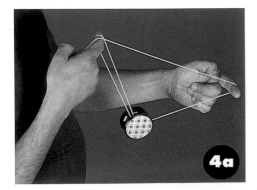

4. With the index finger of your free hand on the inside loop of the yo-yo, follow the string around under the yo-yo, going front to back. This is called a "pass under."

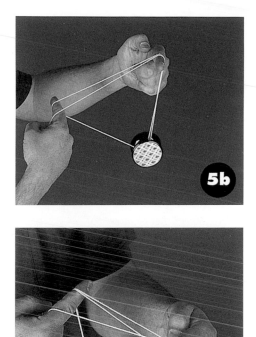

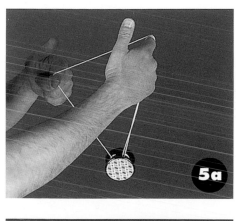

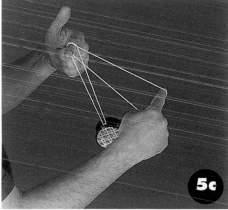

5. When your finger is at about the halfway point on the string closest to you, move it straight across or forward, into the double string. Take the single string, which your yo-yo hand is holding, and pass it under the yo-yo in a back-to-front direction.

6. Punch your finger back into the double string, which will give you another somersault, then roll off your finger the same way you did in Brain Twister and catch it.

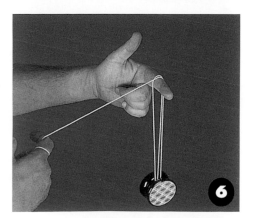

Warp Drive

Grab your dilithium crystals and your yo-yo and get ready to boogie out of here. This looks simple, but it's actually quite challenging.

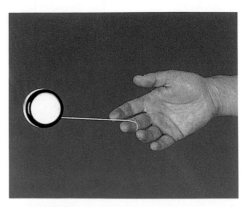

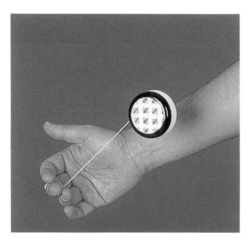

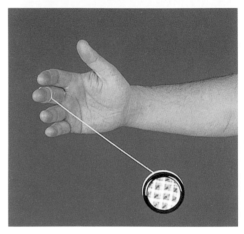

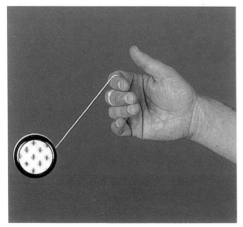

1. Throw a Basic Inside Loop.

2. As it comes back to your hand, give your wrist a hard flick to propel the yo-yo outward into an Around the World.

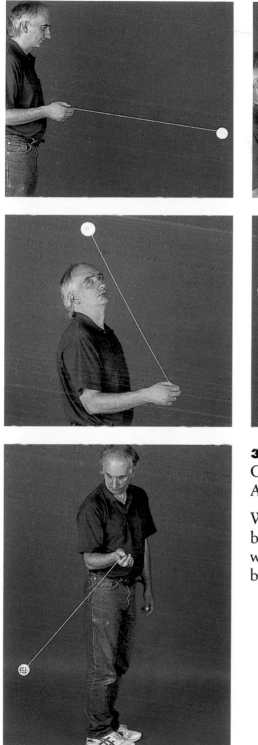

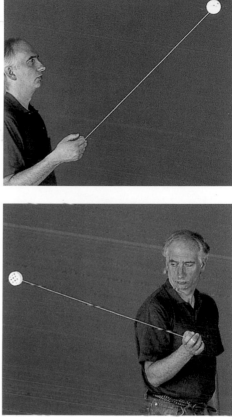

3. Do this again, two more times. Catch the yo-yo after the third Around the World.

Warning: this has the potential to break strings. Make sure you are in a wide-open space with nothing nearby that could be damaged.

Time Warp

The tiny silhouetted figure in the bottom right-hand corner of this book is actually part of a yo-yo movie. Flip the pages of the book and you will see the time warp trick!

1. Throw a forward Around the World.

2. As it completes its rotation and begins to return to your hand, snap your wrist hard, as in Hop the Fence,

which will send the yo-yo into a backward Around the World.

3. As it completes this orbit, bring the yo-yo back to your hand. The fancy term is "regeneration trick."

Two-Handed Tricks

For obvious reasons, you will need two yo-yos for the following tricks. It is recommended that you use two of the same type of yo-yo. Most likely you have only been using your "writing" hand for performing all your tricks. A good way to start is to practice all your basic moves with your other hand. The most important tricks are Hop the Fence and Loops. You'll know you're ready when you can do these without looking at the yo-yo. When you can perform these perfectly, start two-handed yo-yoing.

One expert recommends that you tie your normal yo-yo hand behind you for a week and only practice with your other hand.

Hand behind back

Two-Handed Loops

🪀 🪀 🪀

This one looks really impressive, but will take some time to perfect.

1. Throw a loop with your regular yo-yo hand.

2. As the yo-yo reaches the end of the string, throw the second yo-yo with your other hand. Keep alternating loop throws. The rhythm is an important part of this trick. Relax as you are throwing.

3. Make sure the yo-yo returns are "inside" loops. Practice doing one, then two, then as many as you can without tangling them up.

Two-handed

Milk the Cow

This is an udderly difficult trick to perfect. The trick is to keep the yo-yos moooo-ving.

1. This is simply (and we say that in jest) alternating Hop the Fence. Start by throwing a Hop the Fence with one hand.

3. As each yo-yo returns to your hand, flick your wrist to send the yo-yo back down again.

2. As the yo-yo gets to the bottom of the string, throw the next yo-yo down.

Ride the Horse

👈 👈 👈 👈

Meanwhile, back at the ranch, the two-handed yo-yo kid was ready to get on a pony.

1. Start by performing Inside Loops with your non-yo-yo hand.

2. With your yo-yo hand, throw repetitions of Hop the Fence. Make sure your hops are situated behind your leg, not in front. These motions together resemble a person riding a horse, hence the name.

Loops/Reach for the Moon

This doesn't have an official name; this is just how it's referred to in competition.

1. Using one hand, throw a series of Loops.

2. With the other yo-yo hand (usually your stronger or regular hand), throw a series of Reach for the Moon.

3. The trick to performing this is to be able to do the loops without looking because you need to keep an eye on the hand doing Reach the Moon. If you miss a Loop, it's no big deal. If you miss a Reach for the Moon, you can really hit yourself on the head—usually in the mouth.

Criss Cross

Not a sewing stitch, but a really hard yo-yo maneuver. To give you an idea where your hands should be, hold the yo-yos and cross your hands at the wrists. While you won't be doing this with the yo-yos moving, it gives you an idea of the angle of the yo-yos when they cross each other.

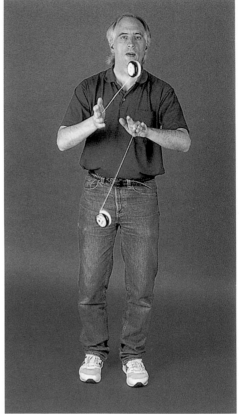

1. Begin by throwing two-handed Loop the Loops.

2. Once you have these moving along cleanly, begin to angle your throws.

3. After several reps, your yo-yos should start to cross each other's paths. Remember when one yo-yo is coming the other is going. This means the yo-yos won't collide in midair. Be prepared for some mishaps while learning this trick.

Whirlwind

A big wind will not blow you away as you attempt this tricky trick. This is not for someone who is easily confused. When you can throw inside/outside Loops with each hand, you are ready.

Start by throwing an inside/ outside Loop.

1. The most important pattern to remember is when one yo-yo is doing an inside loop, the other will follow with an inside loop. You must alternate your throws when you are doing this.

2. Try saying the throw aloud, to help you keep track, i.e., "inside, inside...outside, outside."

Yo-Yo Pictures

Much like the game of "cat's cradle,"
use your yo-yo and string to create
pictures. Afterward, have your string
wind back into your yo-yo.

Eiffel Tower

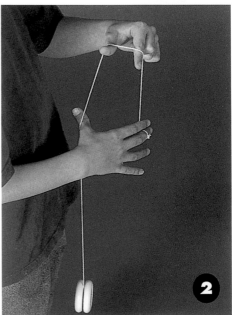

*You don't have to go to Paris to
see the Eiffel Tower. You can make
one of your own.*

1. Throw a fast or hard Sleeper.

2. Using your free hand, join your
index and middle fingers to your
thumb.

3. Place the string between your
body and free hand.

4. Move your yo-yo hand to move
the string over your free hand.

5. As your yo-yo hand comes down,
place your thumb against the string.
Rotate your hands over each other so
the yo-yo hand is on top and the free
hand on the bottom.

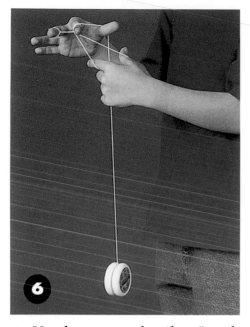

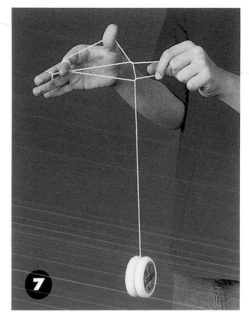

6. You have created a "loop" with your thumb and the fingers of your free hand.

7. Reach through the loop with the two fingers of your free hand, and grasp the hanging string (the one going directly to the yo-yo) and pull that string through the loop, releasing the loop at the same time.

8. Split your hand and fingers to form the "tower."

Motorcycle

You don't need a driver's license to do this trick. If you can do the Eiffel Tower, you've got this trick made.

1. Make the Eiffel Tower. (See above)

2. When you've made the tower, turn it on its side, and "voilà," as they say in France, you have a motorcycle.

3. Allow the yo-yo to spin on the ground, as it does in Walk the Dog, and you now have a moving motorcycle.

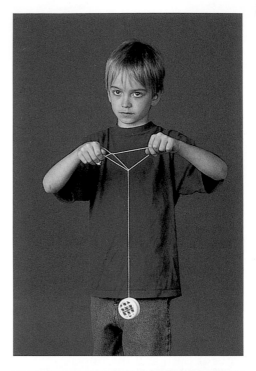

Word "Yo"

Yo Yo Ma is a famous cellist who has not won any yo-yo competitions. But here is a trick you could say was named for him.

1. Make the Eiffel Tower. (See above)

2. Turn your hand over so that the tower is inverted. The yo-yo should be spinning on your left.

3. When viewed head-on, it spells the word "yo."

Jamaican Flag

Jamaican me crazy with this next trick.

1. Throw a fast Sleeper.

2. Using the middle three fingers of your free hand, grasp the string several inches from your yo-yo hand. Hold this hand with the string above your yo-yo hand.

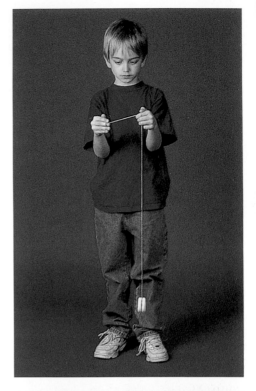

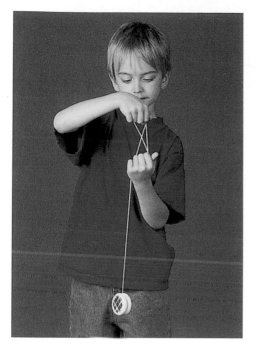

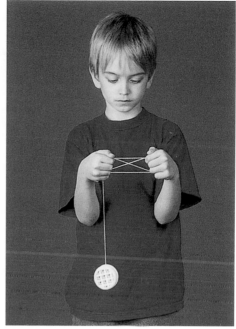

3. Using the middle three fingers of your yo-yo hand, grasp the string several inches from your free hand and pull the string above your free hand.

4. Pull this form sideways and using the pinky of your yo-yo hand, grab the string. When viewed head on, it looks like a flag.

Index